VOLCANOES

Written and edited by **Jenny Wood**

TWO-CAN

VOLCANOES

First published 1990 by
Two-Can Publishing
27 Cowper Street
London EC2A 4AP

© Two-Can Publishing 1990
© Text Jenny Wood 1990
Design by Claire Legemah

Printed in Great Britain

British Library Cataloguing in Publication Data
Wood, Jenny
Volcanoes.
1. Volcanoes
I. Title
551.2'1

ISBN 1-85434-007-7

Photographic Credits:
p. 5 GeoScience Features Picture Library; p.6/7 GeoScience Features Picture Library; p.7 Explorer; p.8 (inset) Frank Lane Picture Agency Ltd; p.8/9 Explorer; p.10 (top) Frank
Lane Picture Agency Ltd, (bottom) Bruce Coleman; p.11 (left) Robert Harding Picture Library, (right) GeoScience Features Picture Library; p.14 Zefa; p.15 GeoScience Features
Picture Library; p.16 (both) Zefa; p.18 Survival Anglia Photo Library; p.19 (top) Rex Features, (bottom) GeoScience Features Picture Library, (right) The Hutchinson Library;
p.20 Explorer; p.22/23 Zefa; p.22 (inset) Ardea; p.23 (left inset) Survival Anglia Photo Library, (right inset) Zefa; Cover photo (front) Zefa; Cover photo (back) Robert Harding
Picture Library.

Illustration Credits:
p.4, 5, 7, 12, 13, 14, 17, 21 Francis Mosley; p.24-28 Linden Artists/Malcolm Stokes

CONTENTS

WHAT IS A VOLCANO?

Volcanoes are openings in the surface of the Earth from which gas and hot molten, or liquid, rock escape and cover the surrounding land. Some volcanoes are simply long cracks in the ground. Others look like cone-shaped mountains with a hole in the top. The hole is called a **vent**.

While the molten rock is inside the Earth, it is known as **magma**. But when it escapes on to the Earth's surface, it is called **lava**. As lava flows, it cools and hardens. The hardened lava, as well as ash and cinders from the volcano, pile up around the vent to create the **cone**.

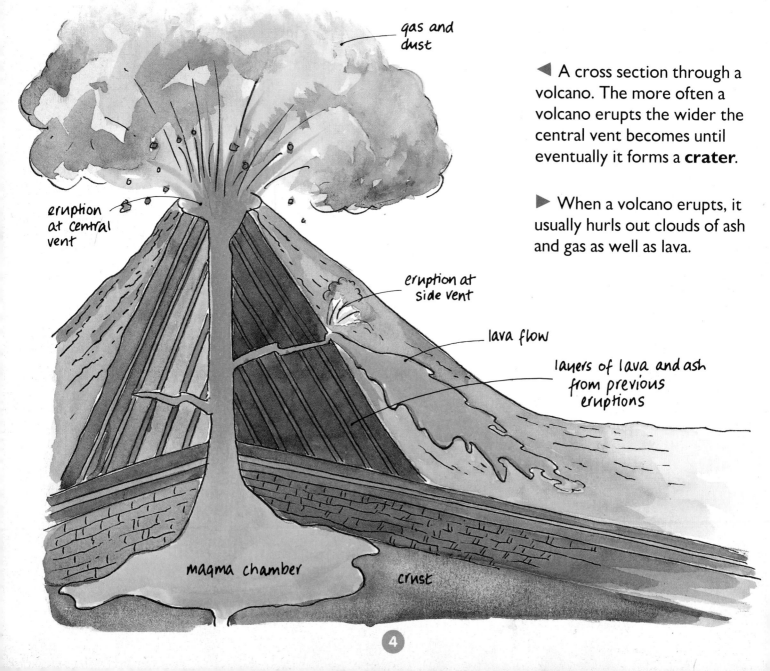

gas and dust

eruption at central vent

◀ A cross section through a volcano. The more often a volcano erupts the wider the central vent becomes until eventually it forms a **crater**.

▶ When a volcano erupts, it usually hurls out clouds of ash and gas as well as lava.

eruption at side vent

lava flow

layers of lava and ash from previous eruptions

magma chamber

crust

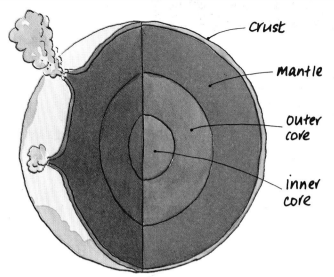

The inside of the Earth is divided into different layers. The thin surface layer, called the **crust**, is made up of slabs, or plates, of rock. These float on a layer of hot, liquid rock called the **mantle**. Next comes the outer **core**, which is made up of hot, liquid metals, and the inner core, which is solid iron.

VOLCANIC ERUPTIONS

A volcanic eruption is a spectacular and often terrifying sight. Red-hot lava may burst out of the volcano with a deafening roar creating beautiful but deadly fire fountains of glowing lava which shoot hundreds of metres into the air. If the lava is very runny it may spill out of openings in the side of the volcano as well as from the central vent and pour down the mountainside in fiery rivers. These lava streams can travel great distances and will burn, bury or flatten anything in their path.

▶ This lava flow from Mauna Loa, one of Hawaii's many volcanoes, is very runny. It will travel a long way before it cools and hardens.

▼ Fire fountains erupt from twin cones on Mount Etna on the island of Sicily. Red-hot lava flows from the mountain's base.

● Stromboli, a volcano off the coast of Italy, erupts once every 20 minutes! It's known as the lighthouse of the Mediterranean.

● On average, between 20 and 30 volcanoes erupt each year.

● Mauna Loa on Hawaii is the largest live volcano on Earth. One eruption lasted for one and a half years!

● The volcanoes on Hawaii, like the one in the diagram below, have wide, gently sloping cones. Because the runny lava from these volcanoes flows and spreads so quickly, the cones do not have the chance to build up to any great height.

THE RISING CLOUD

Sometimes the magma in a volcano is stiff and thick. The gases trapped in it cannot escape easily, so when the eruption comes it is very violent. Sometimes the magma hardens in the pipe leading up to the vent, blocking the flow until the pressure builds up to a point where the whole volcano may be blown apart in one massive explosion. The top of the volcano often collapses into its own magma chamber, forming a large circular crater called a **caldera**.

▶ Eruptions like these can throw out huge clouds of ash which bury the surrounding countryside and destroy animals, plants and even people.

VOLCANIC MATERIALS

Lava is either very runny, or stiff and thick. Different volcanoes produce these different lava types. But some volcanoes produce no liquid lava at all. Instead they shoot out solid pieces of rock. The tiniest pieces are known as **volcanic ash**. The largest ones are called **volcanic bombs**.

Volcanoes may also produce choking clouds of steam and poisonous gases. These can rush down the mountain at over 160 km (100 miles) an hour, smothering the surrounding countryside.

Volcanic dust from eruptions can be spread over a huge area. Dust particles which are carried into the sky may produce brilliant red sunsets in many parts of the world.

▲ This huge area of hardened lava is known as a lava field.

▼ This valley is covered in a thick layer of volcanic dust. As it is washed into the ground, the dust will make the soil very fertile.

▲ **Pumice**, a type of rock light enough to float in water, may be formed when lava cools very quickly. The tiny bubbles are created by gases escaping from the lava as it cools.

▲ As lava cools, it hardens and forms unusual patterns on the ground. Runny lava produces this wrinkled, rope-like surface known as **pahoehoe** (pronounced pa-hoh-ee-hoh-ee).

WHERE VOLCANOES ARE FOUND

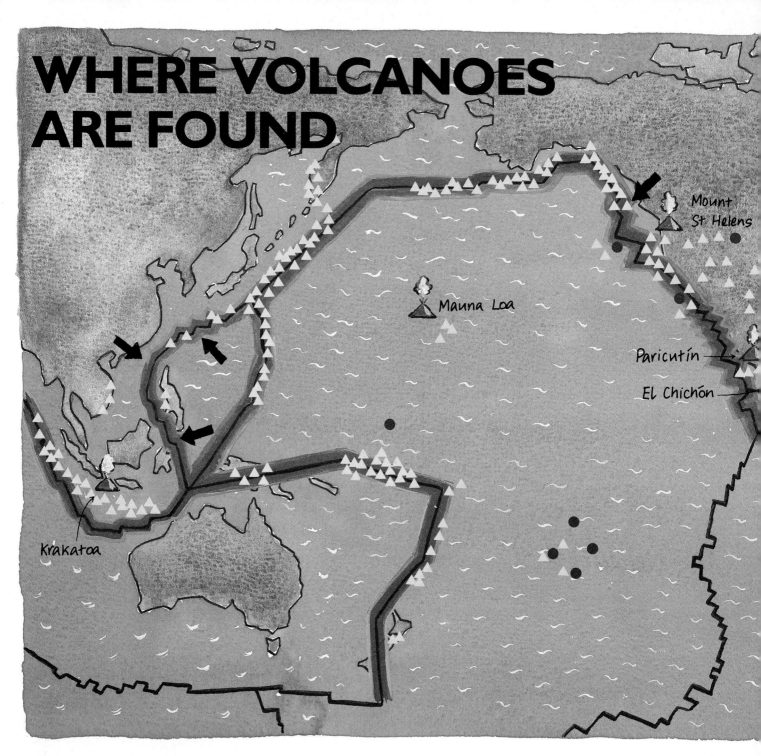

Mount St Helens

Mauna Loa

Paricutín

El Chichón

Krakatoa

The Earth's crust is not solid. It is made up of huge, moving pieces of rock called **plates**, each about 100 km (62 miles) thick. These plates float on the hot liquid rock of the mantle.

Volcanoes usually form where two plates collide and one is forced to slide beneath the other – as, for example, in the so-called **Ring of Fire** around the

▲ This map shows the Earth's plates and also the location of many live volcanoes.

Pacific Ocean. But other volcanoes, such as those in Hawaii, are not caused by plate movement. Instead they form **hotspots**, areas of fierce heat in the mantle which cause magma to bubble up towards the surface.

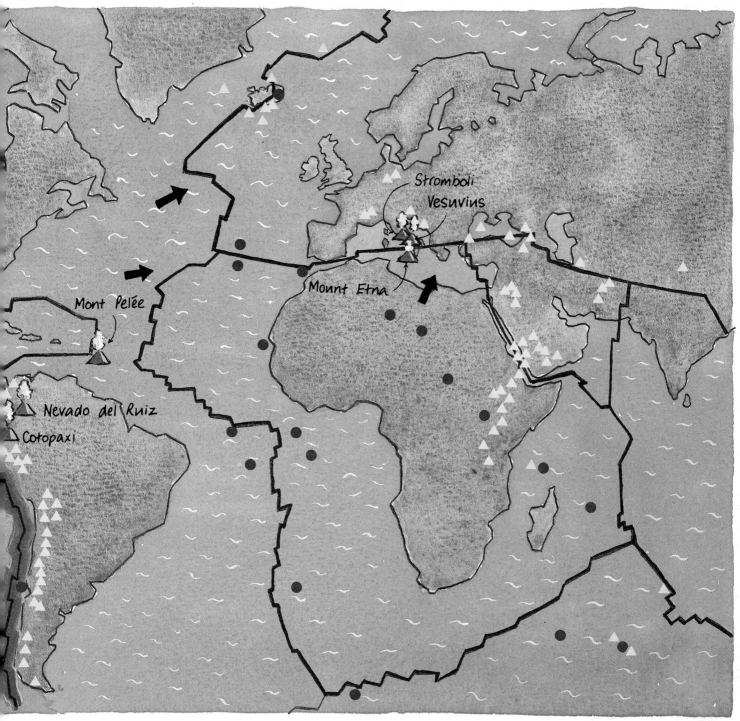

Stromboli
Vesuvius
Mont Pelée
Mount Etna
Nevado del Ruiz
Cotopaxi

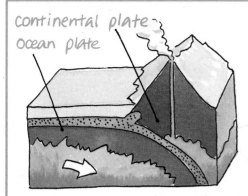

continental plate
ocean plate

When a moving ocean plate collides with a continental plate, it is forced down under the land mass. As it slides, it starts to melt. This creates magma which rises slowly up through the continental plate to create volcanoes.

Key to map

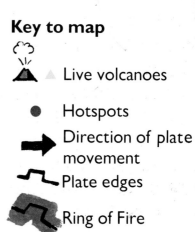

- Live volcanoes
- Hotspots
- Direction of plate movement
- Plate edges
- Ring of Fire

VOLCANIC ISLANDS

Some of the Earth's most spectacular scenery lies beneath the sea. As well as deep trenches and sweeping valleys, there are great mountains which rise from the ocean floor. Many of these mountains are volcanoes. When an underwater volcano erupts, the lava hardens into rock as it meets the water. Repeated eruptions may cause the volcano to build up to such a great height that its tip emerges from the sea.

▼ White Island lies off the eastern coast of New Zealand's North Island, in the so-called Bay of Plenty. There are a number of similar volcanic islands scattered around New Zealand's coastline.

As an underwater volcano explodes, it throws out lava which cools and hardens. A cone-shaped mountain forms around the vent.

The volcano grows with each eruption until its tip is just below sea level. Gas and lava from the next eruption rise above the waves and the tip of the volcano breaks the surface.

The tip of the volcano now lies above sea level. A volcanic island has been born.

In 1963, the crew of a fishing boat off the coast of Iceland saw a column of smoke in the distance. As they sailed closer, billowing clouds of ash and steam began to rise above the waves. The fishermen were witnessing the birth of a volcanic island! As the tip of the new island broke the surface of the water, red-hot lava began to pour from dozens of vents in its cone. That night, the island was 11m (36 feet) high. Four days later, it was as high as two houses, and 650m (2,145 feet) long.

The island was named Surtsey. Scientists came from all over the world to see this exciting event, and to study the growth of animal and plant life. Surtsey kept on growing and changing for almost four years. By 1967, after the last eruption of lava, the island covered more than 2.6 km^2 (1.6 square miles).

▼ Clouds of ash and steam pour from one of the lava vents on Iceland's new volcanic island of Surtsey.

HOT SPRINGS AND GEYSERS

The red-hot magma in the Earth's mantle can create **hot springs** and **geysers**. These are formed where rainwater seeps down into rock above the magma chamber and is then heated. The warm water can bubble back to the surface in the form of a hot spring, or shoot upwards as a jet of steam called a geyser.

Some geysers erupt at regular intervals. A geyser's fountain of steam rises and falls because once the steam has escaped, the geyser pipe refills with water and the process starts all over again.

If the warm water mixes with the soil and chemicals underground, hot mud pools are produced. These boil and bubble on the Earth's surface.

▲ Yellowstone Park in Wyoming, USA, has over 2,500 active geysers and hot springs.

◀ Some people believe that bathing in mud pools can cure certain illnesses.

MAKE A VOLCANO

You will need:

- A small, empty, clean bottle such as an ink bottle or perfume bottle
- A piece of card
- A pin
- A small glass
- Food colouring
- Water

1 Using the pin, make a small hole in the centre of the card.

2 Half-fill the glass with cold water.

3 Put four or five drops of food colouring into the bottle, then fill the bottle with hot water from the tap.

4 Place the card over the top of the glass and hold it in place. Quickly turn the glass over, still holding the card, and place the card and glass on top of the bottle. The water won't fall out as long as you hold the card firmly over the top of the glass. But if you do spill the water, just fill the glass and start again!

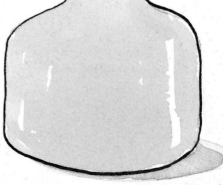

5 Still holding the card, press down gently on the glass. Puffs of colour will rise through the pin-hole into the glass. (Warm water is lighter than cold water, so the warm water rises!)

LIVING NEAR A VOLCANO

Throughout history people have lived near volcanoes. This can be dangerous, as in 1883 when the volcanic island of Krakatoa in Indonesia exploded. The explosion, which was heard 4,800 km (3,000 miles) away, killed 36,000 people on or near the island.

Even when the eruption is not so violent, clouds of poisonous gas can kill people and wildlife over a wide area. This happened in 1986 in West Africa, when carbon dioxide gas poured out from a lake in the crater of a volcano. Lava flows can engulf whole towns. In 1973, the town of Vestmannajyer on the island of Heimaey, Iceland, was buried under tonnes of red-hot lava from an eruption of Eldjfell volcano.

However, there are some advantages to living near a volcano. Volcanic soil is very rich in chemicals which are needed by plants, so it is good for growing vines and food crops such as rice and potatoes. Many important minerals like copper and nickel are mined from volcanic rocks.

▲ A flow of volcanic mud swept through the town of Armero in Colombia, South America, in 1986, killing many people.

▼ The town of Vestmannajyer, Iceland, was overwhelmed by lava in 1973. The islanders sprayed the lava with sea water for five months to try to halt its flow.

► Mineral-rich volcanic soil is perfect for growing rice. Farmers terrace the steep hillsides to prevent the valuable soil being washed away by rain.

◄ These Japanese macaques, or 'snow monkeys', live in the often freezing temperatures and snowy conditions of the high forests of Japan. They keep warm by bathing in hot springs.

TYPES OF VOLCANO

Volcanoes are now classified as being live or dead. A live volcano is one which may erupt in the future. A dead volcano is one which may not erupt in the future. While a live volcano is erupting, it is referred to as **active.** When it is not erupting it is said to be **dormant**.

After an eruption a live volcano may go quiet for a long period. It becomes just like any other mountain. Snow may settle on its summit and there are no signs of life. A live volcano can remain dormant like this for many years. However, deep below the surface, the huge pressure of the magma may build up, and further eruptions may occur many years later.

When a volcano is truly dead, the magma below it sinks back into the depths of the Earth. Eventually the weather wears away the cone until only the **volcanic plug** of solidified lava is left.

▲ Crater Lake, USA. Sometimes the cone of a live volcano collapses inwards forming a huge round crater called a caldera. The caldera can fill with water forming a circular lake. The island seen here is a new volcanic cone.

▲ Eroded volcanic craters on the Galapagos Islands in the Pacific Ocean provide important wildlife habitats for creatures such as this land iguana.

▼ Mount Fuji, the highest mountain in Japan, last erupted in 1707.

▲ The chapel of St Michel d'Aguiche in the French town of Le Puy sits on top of an 80m (260 feet) pillar of rock which was once the central pipe of a volcano.

SCIENCE AT WORK

For years scientists have been trying to find ways of predicting when volcanoes are going to erupt, so that people living in the area have time to reach safety.

Before an eruption, there are often small underground earthquakes, caused by the magma splitting rocks apart as it rises to the surface. An instrument called a **seisometer** helps scientists pinpoint the exact position of the rising magma. In Hawaii, this technique has been so successful that the time and place of eruptions has been forecast accurately.

In the scientific observatory near Mount Etna, scientists can actually hear the magma pouring through pipes within the volcano. As it does so,

▼ Scientists who study volcanoes are called vulcanologists. When they are observing an erupting volcano, they have to wear special heat-resistant suits.

it makes a sort of 'singing' sound. By listening to this 'singing', scientists can follow the magma's movements and try to predict which of the volcano's vents it might break through during the next eruption.

When magma pushes up from below, the sides of a volcano may begin to swell. This causes the ground to tilt. The tilt can be measured using an instrument called a **tiltmeter**, and again this helps scientists to tell where an eruption is going to occur.

Studying volcanic ash can reveal a lot about previous eruptions. Scientists can work out how big they were, how long they lasted, and what areas they affected. It is even possible to calculate the gap between eruptions, and therefore when the next eruption might occur.

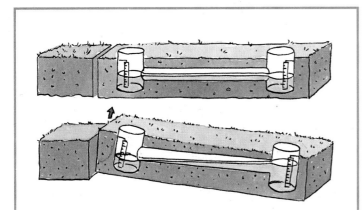

The tiltmeter consists of two containers of liquid, set several metres apart and joined by a tube. If the ground tilts, liquid runs from one container to the other. The change in the levels of the liquid indicates the amount of tilt.

● Scientists now believe that the gas and ash from volcanic eruptions can cause huge changes to the weather by blocking the sun's rays and reducing the world's temperature. In 1816, the eruption of Tambora near Java caused winter weather in the middle of summer in America and Europe. The Americans nicknamed that year 'Eighteen hundred and froze to death'.

● Scientists have developed ways of using the heat inside the Earth's volcanic areas. Most of the houses in Reykjavik, the capital of Iceland, for example, are heated by hot water which is piped from underground heat sources. And power stations in New Zealand, Italy, America, Japan, Mexico and Chile use steam from underground to help generate electricity. Energy from these hot zones below the surface of the Earth is known as **geothermal energy**.

BIRTH OF A VOLCANO

Dionisio Pulido awoke with a start. Dawn was breaking, and sunlight was streaming through the tiny window above his bed. Dionisio lay for a moment, watching and listening, trying to work out what had interrupted his sleep. Suddenly the walls of his hut began to tremble. The floor creaked and groaned as the old wooden planks were disturbed. Even his bed seemed to be moving. Dionisio murmured a silent prayer, asking God to protect him, his family and all the villagers from the strangely angry earth.

It was February 1943. For fifteen days now, the Mexican village of Paricutin where Dionisio lived had been experiencing small earthquakes. Each day the tremors grew a little stronger and more frequent. In one day alone there had been over 500! The villagers were very frightened.

As soon as the tremors stopped,
Dionisio jumped out of bed. He was a
farmer with fields close to the village.
He planned to plough his cornfield
today, ready for the new seed. He must
try to put the earthquakes out of his
mind. He had work to do!

Dionisio hitched his oxen to the
plough and set to work. It was a bitterly
cold day, but Dionisio noticed that the
soil beneath his feet felt quite warm. At
first this puzzled him, but he soon
forgot about it as the hard work of

ploughing began to make him feel
tired and sore.

In one corner of the field there was
an outcrop of rock with a small hollow
in it. This hollow had been there for
as long as Dionisio could remember,
and the village children often
played in it.

As Dionisio neared that corner of the
field, in the late afternoon, he noticed a
crack in the ground by the rock. It
was about 25 metres (80 feet) long,
and went straight through the hollow.

Dionisio walked forwards to look at the crack more carefully. As he did so, he heard a loud, rumbling sound like thunder which seemed to come from beneath his feet. Smoke began to rise from the hollow and the trees at the edge of the field began to sway. Suddenly, the ground around the rock split wide open and bulged up. Dionisio was terrified. As he turned to run, smoke began to pour out of the crack, followed by sparks which set the trees on fire. The smell of sulphur filled the air. Dionisio ran as if the devil were after him! He had no idea that what he was seeing was the birth of a volcano.

As Dionisio raced into the village, shouting at the top of his voice, the villagers gathered quickly to find out what had happened. Dionisio pointed to his field. In the distance, they could now see red-hot rock emerging from a hole at the end of the crack. This hole grew bigger and bigger as they watched.

Some of the villagers stayed up all night, fearful yet fascinated at the same time. Others prayed in the church. At 8 o'clock the following morning, Dionisio went back to his cornfield. He found that a 10 metre (35 feet) high cone had grown overnight – and it was still growing! By midday the cone was about 45 metres (150 feet) high, and by nightfall, red-hot lava was beginning to pour slowly from its base. The next morning, Dionisio had no field left.

That day, those villagers who had not already fled decided it was time to escape. And just in time! During the next week, the volcano grew to a height of 140 metres (460 feet). Fragments of magma were thrown almost a kilometre (half a mile) into the air. The noise of the explosions could be heard in Mexico City, 816 kilometres (510 miles) away.

As the villagers left, scientists began to arrive from all over the world to watch and study this new volcano. The village of Paricutin, and the nearby village of San Juan Parangaricutiro were both destroyed. Vast quantities of volcanic ash covered the countryside for 12 kilometres (20 miles) around. Only the top of the church in San Juan Parangaricutiro could be seen above the lava. Cattle grew thin and died from lack of grazing. Water was scarce because the rivers were clogged with ash and rocks. Birds were overcome by poisonous gases and dropped dead from the sky.

The volcano kept on erupting and growing until 1952. Then 9 years and 52 days after its dramatic birth it grew calm quite suddenly. When Dionisio Pulido brought his grandchildren to visit the spot where he had once lived and worked, the huge cone of volcanic debris stood 410 metres (1,350 feet) above his cornfield. What a story he had to tell them!

TRUE OR FALSE?

Which of these facts are true and which ones are false?
If you have read this book carefully, you will know the answers.

1 All volcanoes are cone-shaped mountains.

2 The Ring of Fire is a volcano on Hawaii.

3 Scientists who study volcanoes are called vulcanologists.

4 The centre of the Earth is known as the crust.

5 Lava is the name given to magma when it escapes on to the Earth's surface.

6 Rice and other food crops grow well in volcanic soil.

7 Volcanic dust can cause red sunsets.

8 Stromboli is the largest live volcano on Earth.

9 A caldera is another name for a magma chamber.

10 The Earth's crust is made up of huge pieces of rock called plates.

11 As runny lava cools and hardens, it produces a wrinkled surface known as pahoehoe.

12 Hotspots are areas on the Earth's surface where volcanoes always form.

13 Volcanic bombs are large pieces of rock which are sometimes thrown out during a volcanic eruption.

GLOSSARY

Active is the word used to describe a live volcano while it is erupting.

Caldera is the huge round crater which forms when the cone of a live volcano collapses inwards.

Cone is the mountain which builds up around a volcano. It is made up of hardened lava, as well as the ash and cinders which are thrown out of the volcano during an explosion.

Core is the name given to the centre of the Earth. It is divided into the outer core, which is made up of hot, liquid metals, and the inner core, which is solid iron.

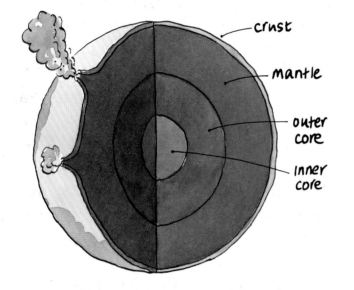

Crater is the hole at the top of a volcano's vent. It widens each time the volcano erupts.

Crust is the name given to Earth's thin surface layer. It is made up of huge, thick slabs of rock called plates which float on the hot, liquid rock of the mantle, the next layer down.

Dormant is the word used to describe a live volcano while it is not erupting.

Geothermal energy is energy which is obtained from the volcanic areas or 'hot zones' below the surface of the Earth.

Geyser is a natural underground spring which shoots up jets of steam on to the surface.

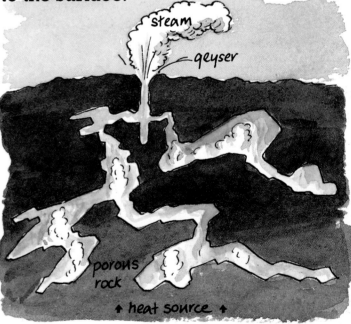

Hot springs are found underground. The warm water they contain bubbles up to the surface.

Hotspot is an area of fierce heat in the Earth's mantle where magma bubbles up to the surface and forms a volcano.

Lava is the name given to magma from inside the Earth when it escapes on to the Earth's surface.

Magma is hot, liquid rock found inside the Earth, in the layer called the mantle.

Mantle is the layer inside the Earth, below the crust. It is made up of hot, liquid rock.

Pahoehoe is the name given to the wrinkled, rope-like surface produced by runny lava as it cools and hardens.

Plate is one of the huge, thick slabs of rock which make up the Earth's crust.

Pumice is a very light type of rock which can float in water. It is formed when lava cools very quickly.

Ring of Fire is the name given to the area around the Pacific Ocean where a large number of the world's live volcanoes are found.

Seisometer is an instrument which can pinpoint the position of rising magma. It is used by scientists to help predict where and when a volcano is going to erupt.

Tiltmeter is an instrument which measures the amount of tilt in the ground caused by magma pushing up from underground and making the sides of a volcano swell. This can help scientists predict where an eruption will occur.

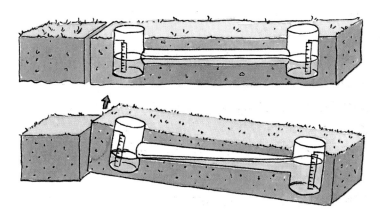

Vent is an opening in a volcano through which magma flows. The main vent is usually in the centre of a volcano, but sometimes there are vents in the sides of a volcano too.

Volcanic ash is the name given to the smallest pieces of rock thrown out of a volcano.

Volcanic bomb is the name given to the largest pieces of rock thrown out of a volcano.

Volcanic plug is the piece of solid lava which remains after weather has worn away a volcano's cone over a period of thousands of years.

INDEX